# STEPHANIE GILMORE

## Women in Sports

MARY HERTZ SCARBROUGH

Rourke
Educational Media

A Division of
Carson
Dellosa
Education

## Before Reading: *Building Background Knowledge and Vocabulary*

Building background knowledge can help children process new information and build upon what they already know. Before reading a book, it is important to tap into what children already know about the topic. This will help them develop their vocabulary and increase their reading comprehension.

### Questions and Activities to Build Background Knowledge:

1. Look at the front cover of the book and read the title. What do you think this book will be about?
2. What do you already know about this topic?
3. Take a book walk and skim the pages. Look at the table of contents, photographs, captions, and bold words. Did these text features give you any information or predictions about what you will read in this book?

### Vocabulary: *Vocabulary Is Key to Reading Comprehension*

Use the following directions to prompt a conversation about each word.

- Read the vocabulary words.
- What comes to mind when you see each word?
- What do you think each word means?

**Vocabulary Words:**
- artistry
- bodyboard
- inequalities
- mentor
- rookie
- wild card

## During Reading: *Reading for Meaning and Understanding*

To achieve deep comprehension of a book, children are encouraged to use close reading strategies. During reading, it is important to have children stop and make connections. These connections result in deeper analysis and understanding of a book.

 Close Reading a Text

During reading, have children stop and talk about the following:

- Any confusing parts
- Any unknown words
- Text to text, text to self, text to world connections
- The main idea in each chapter or heading

Encourage children to use context clues to determine the meaning of any unknown words. These strategies will help children learn to analyze the text more thoroughly as they read.

When you are finished reading this book, turn to the next-to-last page for **After Reading Questions** and an **Activity**.

# TABLE OF CONTENTS

# BORN TO SURF

Stephanie Gilmore grew up near world-class surfing locations in Australia. Stephanie often tagged along with her dad, who loved to surf. At first, she paddled around on a **bodyboard**. By age nine or ten, she was standing on it.

bodyboard

**bodyboard** (BAH-dee-bord): a board used for riding the waves while lying facedown

Young Stephanie quickly became obsessed with surfing. She said:

"It was the first thing I'd think about in the morning and the last thing I thought about when I was going to bed, still covered in sunscreen and saltwater."

### Get to Know Stephanie

- Her nickname is "Happy."
- She was born on January 29, 1988, in Murwillumbah, New South Wales, Australia.
- She has two older sisters.
- She is 5 feet, 10 inches (1.78 meters) tall.

# SURF'S UP

With her father's coaching, Stephanie began competing at age 12. In 2005, she got a **wild card** invitation to a huge competition in Australia. She won! She had another wild card invitation and win in 2006. Her successes qualified her for the World Surf League (WSL) Championship Tour the following year.

**wild card** (wilde kahrd): a person chosen for a competition after all the slots for qualified participants are filled

*Stephanie surfs on a shortboard at a WSL championship event.*

## Shortboards and Longboards

At a length of about 9 feet (2.7 meters), longboards provide stability. They work better than shortboards in less powerful waves. Shortboards are approximately 6 feet (1.8 meters) long. They're better for making quick maneuvers.

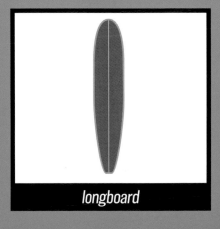

*longboard*

*shortboard*

*Stephanie holds her Association of Surfing Professionals (ASP) World Champion trophy at the Roxy Pro Hawaii.*

WSL Scoring

- Two to four surfers compete in 20- to 35-minute heats.

- Surfers can ride an unlimited number of waves.

- There are five judges.

- Possible scores are 1.00–10.00.

- The two highest-scoring waves determine the surfer's score in the heat.

Stephanie spent 2007 in professional surfing competitions around the world. She competed with other pro surfers for the highest overall score. And at the end of her first season, she had it! She is still the only surfer ever to win the World Championship title as a **rookie**.

*Stephanie surfs during round 12 of the U.S. Open of Surfing.*

**rookie** (RUK-ee): a player in their first year as a professional athlete

Stephanie's rookie win wasn't just luck. She surfed to success with World Championship titles again in 2008, 2009, and 2010. Her four back-to-back world titles set a record for both men and women. She was the favorite to win in 2011 as well. But, her winning streak came to a sudden end.

*Stephanie accepts her 2010 ASP World Title trophy.*

*Stephanie celebrates winning the 2010 ASP Women's World Tour.*

In December 2010, Stephanie was attacked by a man with a history of hurting strangers. Her wrist was broken, and she needed stitches on her head. She couldn't surf for weeks. It took her much longer to get back her peace of mind. She stopped competing and just surfed for fun.

## Life Lessons

According to Stephanie, surfing's lessons can be applied to life.

"There's always going to be another wave. If you fall off and get smashed, you can get back out there and have another chance."

Stephanie trained intensely for the 2012 season. She came back determined and won the World Championship title that year. She won it again in 2014.

Stephanie says the keys to her success are reading the waves and adapting instantly. Her style has been described as pure **artistry** paired with genius precision and technical expertise.

**artistry** (AHR-tis-tree): creative skill or ability

## Unequal Endorsements

Even after her record-setting four World Championship titles, Stephanie faced difficulties. She explained:

"[I]t was a struggle...to get companies...to put up the same kind of cash they were giving to the men."

When Stephanie took first place in a competition in 2007, her take-home award was one-fifth of her male counterpart's.

Stephanie won another World Championship title in 2018. This was her seventh win! It tied her for the women's record.

She has also pushed for equal pay for women surfers. The WSL announced that it would award the same amounts to men and women beginning in 2019. Some **inequalities** still exist, though. For example, women have fewer surfing competitions than men.

**inequalities** (in-i-KWAH-li-teez): situations where some people are treated better or have better opportunities than others

Stephanie is active in Rising Tides, an all-female surfing clinic that encourages girls to become professional surfers. Stephanie never misses an opportunity to **mentor** the girls. Another pro said about Stephanie:

"Not once will she even try and catch a wave. She's just pushing these little girls into waves and getting to know them..."

**mentor** (MEN-tor): to serve as a trusted counselor or guide

Stephanie was one of two women surfers chosen to represent Australia in the 2020 Olympics. This is the first year of surfing as an Olympic sport. In the Olympics, both men and women will compete using shortboards.

# MAKING WAVES ON LAND

Stephanie has also begun making a name for herself in music. She plays the guitar. She has performed with well-known musicians and likes to collect guitars.

Her dad started teaching her to play guitar when she was about nine years old. When she practiced, he would let her get out of doing the dishes.

Stephanie is passionate about environmental issues. She works with Sea Shepherds, an ocean conservation group. Their projects include collecting trash from the ocean and trying to end the use of shark nets.

Australia fought terrible wildfires in 2019 and 2020. Stephanie stepped up to help raise money to support firefighters. She donated a signed surfboard for an online auction. She also played guitar at a two-day fundraiser in January 2020.

Stephanie strives to bring positivity and passion to the things she loves, whether that's music, the environment, or surfing! She said:

"Just being involved in a sport that believes in equality and believes in sending messages that are far greater than just sport and trophies...to me, breathed a whole new life into what I do."

# Memory Game

Look at the pictures. What do you remember

reading on the pages where each image appeared?

# Index

# After Reading Questions

1. Did your understanding of what it takes to be one of the greatest athletes in the world change after reading this book? Explain.

2. What do you think makes Stephanie successful and inspiring?

3. What are two records that Stephanie holds?

4. How did Stephanie help support firefighters battling wildfires in Australia?

5. What issues with pay inequality has Stephanie experienced?

# Activity

Stephanie donates her time to mentor young female surfers through Rising Tides. Have you had a mentor in your life? What have you learned from your mentor? If you haven't had one, imagine what qualities you'd like a mentor to have. Write a thank you note to your mentor or a paragraph describing your ideal mentor.

# About the Author

Mary Hertz Scarbrough loved learning about Stephanie Gilmore and her role in elevating women's surfing. She admires Stephanie's sunny outlook on life, her sheer athleticism, and her commitment to achieving equality in the sport. Mary loves the ocean's pounding surf but lives in land-locked South Dakota.

www.rourkeeducationalmedia.com

Quote sources: Ho, Coco, "An Ode to Stephanie Gilmore," Stab Magazine, July 2019: https://stabmag.com/about-stab/ ; "Aussie surfer Steph Gilmore has her eyes on another world crown," ABC News (Australia), April 2, 2019: https://www.youtube.com/watch?v=4ahkEyrLrd8 ; Roberts, Michael, "How Surfing's Happiest Champ Returned to Center," Februrary 17, 2015: https://www.outsideonline.com/1930246/how-surfings-happiest-champ-returned-center ; Gilmore, Stephanie and Kelly Slater, "Setting the Standard," The Players' Tribune, September 5, 2018: https://www.theplayerstribune.com/en-us/articles/stephanie-gilmore-kelly-slater-setting-the-standard ; Sims, Molly, "Stephanie Gilmore," Humanity Magazine, 2018: https://mag.citizensofhumanity.com/blog/2018/08/24/stephanie-gilmore/

PHOTO CREDITS: page 4: Shutterstock; page 5: Shutterstock; page 6-7: Shutterstock; page 9: Shutterstock, GettyImages; page 10: ©Kirstin Scholtz, ©Shannon Stent / GettyImages; page 11: ©www.iconsmi.com; page 12: Shutterstock, ©Kirstin Scholtz / zumaglobal; page 13: ©Icon Sports Media, Inc.; page 14-15: ©2019 World Surf League; page 16-17: ©Rex Shutterstock; page 18: ©WSL / Sloane, ©Steve Robertson; page 19: ©WSL / Sloane SOCIAL : @wsl @edsloanephoto; page 20: apsphotos © All Rights Reserved; page 20-21: ©2019 World Surf League; page 22-23: ©WSL / Sloane SOCIAL : @wsl @edsloanephoto; page 25: ©2017 MMag Stefan Rotter (Wien, Austria), all rights reserved; page 26-27: GettyImages; page 28: ©Represented by ZUMA Press, Inc.; page 28-29: © WSL / Sloane SOCIAL : @wsl @edsloanephoto

Edited by: Madison Capitano
Cover and interior design by: Rhea Magaro-Wallace

**Library of Congress PCN Data**
Stephanie Gilmore / Mary Hertz Scarbrough
(Women in Sports)
  ISBN 978-1-73163-827-4 (hard cover)
  ISBN 978-1-73163-904-2 (soft cover)
  ISBN 978-1-73163-981-3 (e-Book)
  ISBN 978-1-73164-058-1 (ePub)
Library of Congress Control Number: 2020930271

Rourke Educational Media
Printed in the United States of America
01-1942011937